Love and

MW00915978

This Book Belongs To

o ···································· o
o ···································· o

How To Play

Game for two or more players.
How To Play

1. The first player begins. he/she chooses and reads a question with two possible answers.
2. Other players try to guess what his/her answer is.
3. The first player reveals what answer he/she has chosen and the reason why.
4. Then the second player reads a question...

TIP: You can write players' points when you play play in a larger group.

Would You Rather...

MAKE A VALENTINE'S CARD FOR SOMEONE

OR

RECEIVE ONE?

HAVE A HEART-SHAPED BALLOON

OR

A HEART-SHAPED COOKIE?

Would You Rather...

♥ MAKE A VALENTINE'S CARD FOR ♥
SOMEONE

OR

RECEIVE ONE?

HAVE A HEART-SHAPED BALLOON

OR

A HEART-SHAPED COOKIE?

Would You Rather....

GO ON A VALENTINE'S DAY
PICNIC

OR

HAVE A VALENTINE'S DAY
PARTY?

RECEIVE A BOUQUET OF
FLOWERS

OR

A BOX OF CUPCAKES?

Would You Rather....

PLAY VALENTINE'S DAY GAMES WITH YOUR FRIENDS

OR

FAMILY?

WEAR A RED SHIRT

OR

A PINK SHIRT FOR VALENTINE'S DAY?

Would You Rather....

SHARE A VALENTINE'S TREAT
WITH YOUR FRIEND

OR

EAT IT ALL BY YOURSELF?

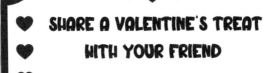

RATHER HAVE A VALENTINE'S
DAY DINNER WITH FAMILY

OR

WITH YOUR FRIENDS?

Would You Rather...

GIVE A VALENTINE'S GIFT TO A FRIEND

OR

A TEACHER?

MAKE A HOMEMADE VALENTINE'S GIFT

OR

BUY ONE?

Would You Rather...

RECEIVE A VALENTINE'S DAY
GIFT WITH A CUTE NOTE

OR

A BIG SURPRISE

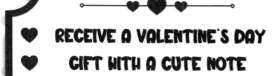

PLAY A VALENTINE'S DAY
SCAVENGER HUNT

OR

A TREASURE HUNT?

Would You Rather...

GET A HUG FROM YOUR
PARENTS

OR

A VALENTINE'S TREAT?

GIVE YOUR VALENTINE'S TREAT
TO SOMEONE ELSE

OR

KEEP IT FOR YOURSELF?

Would You Rather....

CELEBRATE VALENTINE'S DAY WITH CANDY

OR

WITH CRAFTS?

HAVE A VALENTINE'S DAY PARTY WITH LOTS OF DECORATIONS

OR

WITH LOTS OF TREATS?

Would You Rather...

RECEIVE A TEDDY BEAR

OR

A HEART-SHAPED PILLOW?

WRITE A POEM FOR VALENTINE'S DAY

OR

DRAW A PICTURE FOR SOMEONE?

Would You Rather...

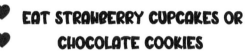

EAT STRAWBERRY CUPCAKES OR
CHOCOLATE COOKIES

OR

VALENTINE'S DAY?

HAVE A VALENTINE'S DAY
SLEEPOVER

OR

A VALENTINE'S PARTY?

Would You Rather...

GET A VALENTINE'S GIFT FROM A FRIEND

OR

FROM A FAMILY MEMBER?

GIVE SOMEONE A VALENTINE'S CARD WITH STICKERS

OR

GLITTER?

Would You Rather...

HAVE A VALENTINE'S DAY FULL OF SURPRISES

OR

KNOW EVERYTHING IN ADVANCE?

RECEIVE A HAND-MADE VALENTINE'S CARD

OR

A STORE-BOUGHT ONE?

Would You Rather...

RATHER GO TO A VALENTINE'S DAY DANCE

OR

TO A VALENTINE'S DAY PICNIC?

GIVE A VALENTINE'S DAY CARD TO YOUR PET

OR

TO YOUR TEACHER?

Would You Rather...

GIVE SOMEONE FLOWERS

OR

CHOCOLATES ON VALENTINE'S DAY?

RECEIVE A HEART-SHAPED BALLOON

OR

A HEART-SHAPED CAKE?

Would You Rather....

SEND A VALENTINE'S DAY CARD
TO SOMEONE YOU LOVE

OR

OR TO SOMEONE WHO'S YOUR
FRIEND?

EAT PINK CAKE

OR

HEART-SHAPED COOKIES?

Would You Rather...

MAKE VALENTINE'S DAY COOKIES

OR

VALENTINE'S DAY BROWNIES?

DO A VALENTINE'S DAY CRAFT

OR

SING A VALENTINE'S DAY SONG?

Would You Rather...

HAVE HEART-SHAPED PANCAKES

OR

HEART-SHAPED WAFFLES?

GIVE YOUR VALENTINE'S CARD TO YOUR FAMILY

OR

TO YOUR FRIENDS?

Would You Rather...

MAKE VALENTINE'S DAY DECORATIONS WITH PAPER

OR

WITH FABRIC?

CREATE A BIG HEART-SHAPED DRAWING

OR

A BIG HEART-SHAPED SCULPTURE?

Would You Rather....

DECORATE COOKIES WITH ICING

OR

WITH SPRINKLES FOR VALENTINE'S DAY?

EAT CHOCOLATE-COVERED STRAWBERRIES

OR

PINK COTTON CANDY ON VALENTINE'S DAY?

Would You Rather...

SPEND VALENTINE'S DAY WITH YOUR FAMILY

OR

WITH YOUR BEST FRIEND?

RECEIVE A VALENTINE'S DAY GIFT WITH A SMILEY FACE

OR

WITH HEARTS?

Would You Rather...

MAKE A VALENTINE'S CARD WITH CRAYONS

OR

WITH MARKERS?

DECORATE YOUR HOUSE WITH BALLOONS

OR

STREAMERS FOR VALENTINE'S DAY?

Would You Rather...

RECEIVE A VALENTINE'S HUG

OR

A VALENTINE'S HIGH-FIVE?

GO ICE SKATING

OR

ROLLER SKATING ON VALENTINE'S DAY?

Would You Rather....

HAVE A VALENTINE'S DAY
BREAKFAST WITH PANCAKES

OR

CEREAL?

GO ON A VALENTINE'S DAY
TREASURE HUNT

OR

PLAY A GAME OF CHARADES?

Would You Rather...

MAKE A VALENTINE'S DAY CROWN

OR

A VALENTINE'S DAY NECKLACE?

GIVE A HEART-SHAPED CHOCOLATE

OR

A HEART-SHAPED CANDY?

Would You Rather....

SEND A VALENTINE'S DAY CARD TO SOMEONE WHO MAKES YOU LAUGH

OR

TO SOMEONE WHO MAKES YOU SMILE?

RATHER CELEBRATE VALENTINE'S DAY WITH A PARTY

OR

WITH A QUIET EVENING AT HOME?

Would You Rather...

♥ **MAKE VALENTINE'S DAY CARDS** ♥
FOR YOUR FRIENDS

OR

FOR YOUR FAMILY?

♥ **GET A VALENTINE'S GIFT IN A** ♥
HEART-SHAPED BOX

OR

A HEART-SHAPED BAG?

Would You Rather....

GIVE A VALENTINE'S DAY GIFT TO A SIBLING

OR

A PARENT?

DECORATE CUPCAKES WITH PINK ICING E WITH BALLOONS

OR

RED ICING?

Would You Rather...

WRITE A VALENTINE'S POEM

OR

SING A VALENTINE'S SONG?

SPEND VALENTINE'S DAY AT THE BEACH

OR

AT THE PARK?

Would You Rather....

RECEIVE A VALENTINE'S CARD WITH HEARTS

OR

WITH STARS?

RECEIVE A TEDDY BEAR WITH A BOWTIE

OR

ONE WITH A SCARF?

Would You Rather...

SPEND VALENTINE'S DAY WITH A
FUN ACTIVITY

OR

A RELAXING ACTIVITY?

RECEIVE A VALENTINE'S DAY
GIFT THAT'S HANDMADE

OR

STORE-BOUGHT?

Would You Rather...

HAVE VALENTINE'S DAY SNACKS WITH LOTS OF COLORS

OR

WITH LOTS OF SWEETNESS?

WRITE A FUNNY VALENTINE'S DAY JOKE

OR

A SWEET VALENTINE'S DAY MESSAGE?

Would You Rather...

GIVE A VALENTINE'S DAY GIFT TO A FRIEND TH CRAYONS

OR

A TEACHER?

GET A VALENTINE'S CARD WITH CUTE ANIMALS

OR

WITH COLORFUL HEARTS?

Would You Rather...

RECEIVE A BALLOON BOUQUET

OR

A CANDY BOUQUET?

MAKE A HEART-SHAPED PIZZA

OR

HEART-SHAPED COOKIES FOR VALENTINE'S DAY?

Would You Rather...

RECEIVE A VALENTINE'S GIFT WITH YOUR FAVORITE COLOR

OR

WITH A FUN DESIGN?

PLAY A VALENTINE'S DAY TRIVIA GAME

OR

A VALENTINE'S DAY GUESSING GAME?

Would You Rather...

♥ EAT YOUR VALENTINE'S CANDY ♥
ALL AT ONCE

OR

SAVE SOME FOR LATER?

MAKE A VALENTINE'S DAY CARD
WITH A RAINBOW

OR

WITH FLOWERS?

Would You Rather...

RECEIVE A VALENTINE'S DAY GIFT WITH LOTS OF SPARKLES

OR

WITH LOTS OF HEARTS?

RECEIVE A RED ROSE OR A PINK TULIP

OR

VALENTINE'S DAY?

Would You Rather....

MAKE A VALENTINE'S DAY BANNER

OR

VALENTINE'S DAY CENTERPIECE?

SEND A VALENTINE'S CARD TO SOMEONE WHO IS KIND

OR

TO SOMEONE WHO IS FUNNY?

Would You Rather...

GIVE SOMEONE A HEART-SHAPED CARD

OR

A HEART-SHAPED BOX?

A VALENTINE'S DAY ART PROJECT

OR

A VALENTINE'S DAY SCIENCE EXPERIMENT?

Would You Rather...

EAT VALENTINE'S DAY CUPCAKES
WITH LOTS OF FROSTING

OR

LOTS OF SPRINKLES?

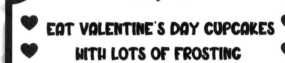

HAVE HEART-SHAPED STICKERS

OR

HEART-SHAPED STAMPS FOR
VALENTINE'S DAY?

Would You Rather....

SPEND VALENTINE'S DAY MAKING CRAFTS

OR

PLAYING GAMES?

HAVE A VALENTINE'S DAY DANCE PARTY

OR

A VALENTINE'S DAY MOVIE NIGHT?

Would You Rather...

GET A VALENTINE'S DAY HUG
FROM YOUR TEACHER

OR

FROM YOUR FRIEND?

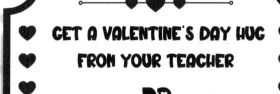

RECEIVE A VALENTINE'S DAY
GIFT THAT SMELLS NICE

OR

THAT LOOKS PRETTY?

Would You Rather...

MAKE A VALENTINE'S DAY POSTER

OR

A VALENTINE'S DAY CARD?

SHARE YOUR VALENTINE'S DAY TREATS

OR

KEEP THEM ALL FOR YOURSELF?

Would You Rather...

PLAY VALENTINE'S DAY MUSICAL CHAIRS

OR

VALENTINE'S DAY FREEZE DANCE?

MAKE A VALENTINE'S DAY HEART-SHAPED BOOKMARK

OR

A VALENTINE'S DAY HEART-SHAPED CARD?

Would You Rather....

DECORATE YOUR SCHOOL DESK WITH HEARTS

OR

WITH STARS FOR VALENTINE'S DAY?

RECEIVE A VALENTINE'S GIFT THAT'S SOFT

OR

ONE THAT'S SQUISHY?

Would You Rather...

GO ON A VALENTINE'S DAY
SCAVENGER HUNT

OR

A VALENTINE'S DAY NATURE
WALK?

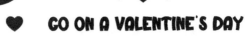

GET A VALENTINE'S CARD FROM
YOUR GRANDMA

OR

YOUR AUNT?

Would You Rather...

MAKE A VALENTINE'S CARD WITH CRAYONS

OR

WITH MARKERS?

SPEND VALENTINE'S DAY READING LOVE STORIES

OR

MAKING CRAFTS?

Would You Rather...

RECEIVE A VALENTINE'S GIFT WITH GLITTER

OR

WITH RIBBONS?

CREATE A VALENTINE'S DAY DANCE

OR

SING A VALENTINE'S SONG?

Would You Rather...

MAKE A VALENTINE'S DAY
DRAWING WITH LOTS OF HEARTS

OR

WITH LOTS OF STARS?

PLAY VALENTINE'S DAY BINGO

OR

VALENTINE'S DAY PICTIONARY?

Would You Rather...

RECEIVE A HEART-SHAPED CHOCOLATE

OR

A BOX OF CANDY HEARTS?

MAKE A VALENTINE'S DAY CROWN

OR

A VALENTINE'S DAY BRACELET?

Would You Rather...

EAT HEART-SHAPED PANCAKES

OR

WAFFLES ON VALENTINE'S DAY?

SEND A VALENTINE'S DAY
LETTER TO YOUR MOM

OR

DAD?

Would You Rather...

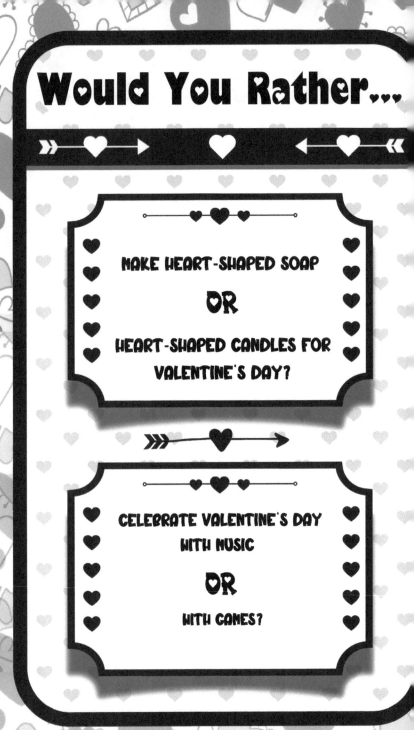

MAKE HEART-SHAPED SOAP

OR

HEART-SHAPED CANDLES FOR VALENTINE'S DAY?

CELEBRATE VALENTINE'S DAY WITH MUSIC

OR

WITH GAMES?

Would You Rather....

GIVE YOUR VALENTINE'S CARD TO A CLASSMATE

OR

A SIBLING?

HAVE A HEART-SHAPED SANDWICH

OR

A HEART-SHAPED SNACK?

Would You Rather...

DECORATE YOUR VALENTINE'S DAY CARD WITH GLITTER

OR

WITH STICKERS?

RECEIVE A VALENTINE'S DAY TREAT THAT'S SOUR

OR

THAT'S SWEET?

Would You Rather....

RECEIVE A VALENTINE'S DAY TEDDY BEAR

OR

A VALENTINE'S DAY BUNNY?

SPEND VALENTINE'S DAY MAKING A SCRAPBOOK

OR

A PHOTO ALBUM?

Would You Rather...

GIVE A HEART-SHAPED NECKLACE

OR

A HEART-SHAPED KEYCHAIN FOR VALENTINE'S DAY?

RECEIVE A VALENTINE'S CARD WITH GLITTER

OR

WITH SHINY PAPER?

Would You Rather...

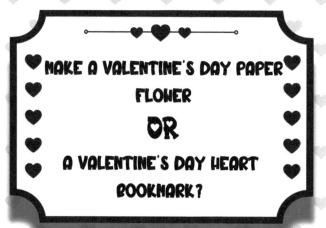

MAKE A VALENTINE'S DAY PAPER FLOWER

OR

A VALENTINE'S DAY HEART BOOKMARK?

GET A VALENTINE'S GIFT WITH LOTS OF COLORS

OR

LOTS OF HEARTS?

Would You Rather...

CELEBRATE VALENTINE'S DAY WITH FUN GAMES WITH FAMILY

OR

WITH FRIENDS?

MAKE AN AMAZING VALENTINE'S CARD FOR YOUR FRIENDS

OR

WRITE THEN A SWEET MESSAGE?

Would You Rather...

MAKE VALENTINE'S DAY
DECORATIONS WITH BALLOONS

OR

WITH STREAMERS?

SPEND VALENTINE'S DAY BAKING
TREATS

OR

MAKING CARDS?

Would You Rather...

RECEIVE A VALENTINE'S DAY
GIFT THAT'S A TOY

OR

A BOOK?

RECEIVE A VALENTINE'S DAY
LETTER FROM A FRIEND

OR

FROM A PARENT?

Would You Rather...

PLAY VALENTINE'S DAY BOARD GAMES

OR

VALENTINE'S DAY CARD GAMES?

GIVE SOMEONE A VALENTINE'S DAY PRESENT WRAPPED WITH RED PAPER

OR

PINK PAPER?

Would You Rather...

MAKE VALENTINE'S DAY CRAFTS
WITH FRIENDS

OR

WITH FAMILY?

DECORATE VALENTINE'S DAY
COOKIES WITH SPRINKLES

OR

FROSTING?

Would You Rather...

♥ MAKE A VALENTINE'S DAY CARD ♥
WITH YOUR HANDPRINTS

OR

WITH YOUR FINGERPRINTS?

SEND A VALENTINE'S DAY
MESSAGE TO YOUR PET

OR

TO YOUR BEST FRIEND?

Would You Rather...

MAKE A VALENTINE'S DAY PUPPET

OR

A VALENTINE'S DAY CARD?

CELEBRATE VALENTINE'S DAY WITH FAMILY

OR

WITH FRIENDS?

Would You Rather...

MAKE VALENTINE'S DAY
DECORATIONS WITH PAPER

OR

FABRIC?

RECEIVE A HEART-SHAPED
CAKE

OR

A BOX OF HEART-SHAPED
COOKIES?

Would You Rather...

MAKE A VALENTINE'S DAY CARD

OR

A VALENTINE'S DAY CROWN?

SEND A VALENTINE'S DAY CARD TO A TEACHER

OR

TO A FRIEND?

Would You Rather...

SPEND VALENTINE'S DAY AT HOME

OR

AT A FRIEND'S HOUSE?

DECORATE A VALENTINE'S DAY TREE

OR

A VALENTINE'S DAY TABLE?

Would You Rather...

RECEIVE A HEART-SHAPED PENCIL

OR

A HEART-SHAPED ERASER?

MAKE VALENTINE'S DAY DECORATIONS WITH GLUE

OR

WITH TAPE?

Would You Rather...

HAVE A VALENTINE'S DAY PARTY

OR

A VALENTINE'S DAY PICNIC?

GET A VALENTINE'S DAY GIFT THAT'S A NECKLACE

OR

A BRACELET?

Would You Rather...

❤ MAKE A VALENTINE'S DAY CARD ❤
FOR SOMEONE IN SCHOOL

OR

OR FOR A FAMILY MEMBER?

RECEIVE A VALENTINE'S DAY
CARD WITH A CUTE PUPPY

OR

A CUTE KITTEN?

Would You Rather....

MAKE A VALENTINE'S DAY CARD
FOR YOUR BEST FRIEND

OR

YOUR SIBLING?

GET A VALENTINE'S DAY CARD
WITH HEARTS

OR

WITH FLOWERS?

Would You Rather...

CREATE A VALENTINE'S DAY DANCE

OR

A VALENTINE'S DAY STORY?

MAKE A HEART-SHAPED PIZZA

OR

A HEART-SHAPED CAKE FOR VALENTINE'S DAY?

Would You Rather....

GO ROLLER SKATING OR ICE SKATING 'S A TOY

OR

VALENTINE'S DAY?

RECEIVE A VALENTINE'S DAY GIFT WITH SPARKLES

OR

WITH GLITTER?

Would You Rather...

DECORATE YOUR VALENTINE'S DAY TREATS WITH CHOCOLATE

OR

WITH FROSTING?

GIVE SOMEONE A VALENTINE'S DAY CARD

OR

A VALENTINE'S DAY GIFT?

Would You Rather....

MAKE A VALENTINE'S DAY NECKLACE

OR

A VALENTINE'S DAY BRACELET?

SEND A VALENTINE'S CARD TO A FRIEND

OR

A RELATIVE?

Would You Rather...

DECORATE A HEART-SHAPED BALLOON

OR

A HEART-SHAPED CARD?

RECEIVE A HEART-SHAPED LOLLIPOP

OR

A VALENTINE'S DAY COOKIE?

Would You Rather...

MAKE VALENTINE'S DAY CARDS
WITH GLITTER

OR

WITH STAMPS?

GET A VALENTINE'S DAY GIFT
THAT'S BIG E'S DAY LETTER FROM
A FRIEND

OR

ONE THAT'S SMALL BUT SPECIAL?

Would You Rather....

DECORATE A VALENTINE'S DAY BAG

OR

A VALENTINE'S DAY BOX?

RECEIVE A VALENTINE'S DAY TREAT THAT'S CHOCOLATE

OR

FRUIT-FLAVORED?

Would You Rather...

CELEBRATE VALENTINE'S DAY
WITH GAMES

OR

WITH ACTIVITIES?

RECEIVE A VALENTINE'S GIFT
WITH RIBBONS

OR

WITH GLITTER?

Would You Rather...

HAVE A VALENTINE'S DAY STORY READ TO YOU

OR

A VALENTINE'S DAY SONG SUNG TO YOU?

RECEIVE A HEART-SHAPED CARD

OR

A HEART-SHAPED COOKIE?

Would You Rather...

CREATE A VALENTINE'S DAY PICTURE WITH MARKERS

OR

WITH CRAYONS?

RECEIVE A VALENTINE'S DAY GIFT THAT'S A PUZZLE

OR

A TOY?

Would You Rather....

SEND A VALENTINE'S DAY CARD TO SOMEONE WHO MAKES YOU LAUGH

OR

SOMEONE WHO MAKES YOU HAPPY?

MAKE A VALENTINE'S DAY DRAWING

OR

A VALENTINE'S DAY CRAFT?

Would You Rather...

CELEBRATE VALENTINE'S DAY WITH TREATS

OR

WITH DECORATIONS?

GET A VALENTINE'S DAY CARD WITH SPARKLES

OR

WITH HEARTS?

Would You Rather...

HAVE HEART-SHAPED TREATS

OR

ROUND TREATS FOR VALENTINE'S DAY?

DECORATE YOUR VALENTINE'S DAY CARD WITH RIBBONS

OR

WITH GLITTER?

Would You Rather...

RECEIVE A HEART-SHAPED PILLOW

OR

A VALENTINE'S DAY PLUSH?

GO TO A VALENTINE'S DAY CARNIVAL

OR

A VALENTINE'S DAY PARADE?

Would You Rather...

MAKE A HEART-SHAPED GIFT

OR

A HEART-SHAPED CARD FOR SOMEONE SPECIAL?

DECORATE YOUR ROOM WITH VALENTINE'S DAY HEARTS

OR

WITH VALENTINE'S DAY FLOWERS?

Would You Rather...

CELEBRATE VALENTINE'S DAY
WITH FUN ACTIVITIES

OR

WITH RELAXING ACTIVITIES?

PLAY VALENTINE'S DAY GAMES

OR

MAKE VALENTINE'S DAY
DECORATIONS?

Would You Rather...

GET A VALENTINE'S GIFT THAT'S A TOY

OR

ONE THAT'S A CRAFT KIT?

MAKE A VALENTINE'S DAY BOOK

OR

A VALENTINE'S DAY PICTURE FRAME?

Would You Rather...

GO TO A VALENTINE'S DAY ICE CREAM PARTY

OR

A VALENTINE'S DAY CUPCAKE PARTY?

RECEIVE A VALENTINE'S DAY GIFT THAT'S A SOFT TOY

OR

A FUN GAME?

Would You Rather...

MAKE VALENTINE'S DAY CARDS
FOR YOUR CLASSMATES

OR

FOR YOUR FAMILY?

HAVE VALENTINE'S DAY SNACKS
WITH CHOCOLATE

OR

WITH FRUIT?

Would You Rather...

DECORATE VALENTINE'S DAY CUPCAKES WITH ICING

OR

SPRINKLES?

MAKE VALENTINE'S DAY CRAFTS WITH GLUE

OR

WITH TAPE?

Would You Rather...

GO TO A VALENTINE'S DAY FAIR

OR

TO A VALENTINE'S DAY CONCERT?

RECEIVE A VALENTINE'S DAY GIFT WITH A SWEET MESSAGE

OR

A FUNNY ONE?

Would You Rather...

PLAY VALENTINE'S DAY GAMES
WITH YOUR PARENTS

OR

WITH YOUR FRIENDS?

HAVE A VALENTINE'S DAY GIFT
THAT'S A TOY

OR

A VALENTINE'S DAY TREAT?

Would You Rather....

♥GET A VALENTINE'S CARD FROM A♥
NEIGHBOR

OR

FROM A RELATIVE?

SPEND VALENTINE'S DAY WITH A
FUN ACTIVITY

OR

A QUIET ACTIVITY?

Would You Rather....

♥ MAKE A VALENTINE'S DAY CARD ♥
WITH STICKERS

OR

WITH GLITTER?

HAVE HEART-SHAPED PANCAKES

OR

HEART-SHAPED WAFFLES?

Would You Rather....

♥ DECORATE YOUR VALENTINE'S ♥
DAY CARD WITH CRAYONS

OR

MARKERS?

♥ HAVE A VALENTINE'S DAY TREAT ♥
WITH PINK ICING

OR

RED ICING?

Would You Rather...

GIVE A VALENTINE'S DAY GIFT TO YOUR SIBLING

OR

TO YOUR PET?

RECEIVE A VALENTINE'S DAY GIFT WITH YOUR FAVORITE COLOR

OR

YOUR FAVORITE SHAPE?

Would You Rather....

DECORATE YOUR ROOM WITH HEARTS

OR

WITH STARS FOR VALENTINE'S DAY?

CREATE A VALENTINE'S DAY DANCE

OR

VALENTINE'S DAY SONG?

Would You Rather...

HAVE A VALENTINE'S DAY FILLED WITH FUN

OR

WITH SURPRISES?

SEND A VALENTINE'S CARD FILLED WITH FLOWERS

OR

FILLED WITH HEARTS?

Made in United States
Troutdale, OR
01/10/2025

27808974R00060